Who's Who
In
Grandpa's Zoo

A to Z

Who's Who
in
Grandpa's Zoo

by Jerry Norton

Who's Who In Grandpa's Zoo

Published by Gatekeeper Press
7853 Gunn Hwy., Suite 209
Tampa, FL 33626
www.GatekeeperPress.com

ISBN (hardcover): 9781662942211

Preface

Of the millions of creatures in the animal kingdom—both existing and pre-historic—only fifty-eight are featured in this first edition of *Who's Who In Grandpa's Zoo*. Their portraits are all products of the author's palette.

Two of those fifty-eight creatures, the Xanado and its cousin the Xanadon't (aka Gnosh, Grox, Konoc, or Porcoo) are the mystical products of SporeWiki, a collaborative encyclopedia dedicated to Spore, the simulation game that was developed by Will Wright. These two creatures are used here under the Creative Commons Attribution-Share Alike License.

Except for the Xanado and Xanadont, all the other animals in this book lived on this earth at some time. In addition, all but one of the verses associated with these fifty-eight animals are products of the author's imagination. The lone exception is **The Pelican's** limerick which was written by D.L. Merritt on January 11, 1972.

This is the third in the author's **"from my palette series"**.

to

Prologue

Some extraordinary creatures
can be found in Grandpa's Zoo.
The Aardvark and the Zebu
come to mind--to name a few.
There is also Deodicurus
(it's a dinosaur that's fat),
And a yellow-banded dart frog
and a scary vampire bat.
And don't forget the Ibex
or the Emu and the Gnu.
Just a few of the surprises
you will find in Grandpa's Zoo

The Aardvark

The Aardvark, for certain,
is not very pretty.
It resembles a creature
designed by committee.
With ears like a rabbit,
the snout of a pig
And a kangaroo tail
that is almost too big.
To top it all off,
it is covered with hair,
And they walk on their toes
when they go anywhere.

The Amargasaurus

This is Amargasaurus--
a terrifying sight.
It scared me half to death
before I woke up late last night.

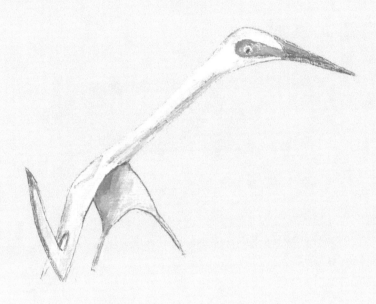

The Arambourgiania

Behold this pterodactyl--
it's a pre-historic bird.
To think that they could ever fly
is patently absurd.

The Assassin Bug

Assassin Bugs and Kissing Bugs,
they're practically the same.
It's best if you avoid them both,
regardless of their name.

The Axolotl

This happy salamander
with a face like Aristotle
To know what it is smiling at--
please ask the Axolotl.

B

The Babirusa

The homely babirusa
is a special kind of pig.
Its teeth and tusks are known
to grow so very, very big.
The tusks may grow a foot or more--
right back into its head.
Which often leaves the babirusa
very, very dead.

B

The Blue Iguana

"Why," you may be asking,
"Is this Iguana blue?"
With a face like an Iguana,

You'd be feeling that way too.

B

The Bumble Bee

Was there any expectation
that this cotton ball could fly?
Of course, it can't. It never could--
now please don't ask me why!

The Caiman

It's hard to tell a caiman
from a gator or a croc.
But a bite by any one's the same--
a severe, unpleasant shock.

The Cassowary

This beautiful bird
never learned how to fly.
Without any wings,
you can understand why.

The Laughing Cat
A playful sense of humor's
found in every single cat.
The challenge is to find out what
this tabby's laughing at.

East African Crowned Crane

One thing about this special pair
I cannot ascertain.
I'm certain though, that they will know,
Which one's the momma crane?

The Dilophosaurus

This creature earned an Oscar.
starring in *Jurassic Park*.
I'd surely hate to meet it,
all alone and after dark.

D

The Doedicurus

This is a Doedicurus,
a creature rather frail.
Except for all those pointed spikes
and very lethal tail.

D

The Douc

This "Costumed Ape" is noted for its wardrobe,
bright and gay.
Too bad the Douc is forced to wear
the same thing every day.

The Dunkleosteous

When Denvon the Dunkle
would come out to play,
It goes without saying,
NO SWIMMING TODAY!!

E

The Electric Eel

Avoid all close encounters
with the feared electric eel.
Or you will find how tasing
with a Taser gun might feel.

The Emu

The emu is another of the big birds
that can't fly.
Because their wings are way too small,
they hardly ever try.
Instead, as runners, they are now extremely fleet.
At 50 miles per hour,
they are very hard to beat.

F

The Fallow Deer

The winner of the antler prize--
in case you haven't guessed
This Fallow Deer--It is the one
that Santa likes the best.

The Firefly

What fun--as kids--we used to have,
(if bedtime we'd eluded)
In catching jars of fireflies
(their batteries included).

G

Gila-Monster

The Gila monster only eats
but several times a year.
So, when it dines, I think you'll find
it's best if you stay clear.

The Gnu

The **Wildebeest,** it seems,
is now the new name for the **Gnu.**
The **Gnu,** I'm sure,
would much prefer
his old name to his new.
Wouldn't you?

G

The Golden Lion Tamarin

The Golden Lion Tamarin's
a monkey, not a cat.
It's called a lion just because
it looks so much like that.

The Gorilla

The Gorilla is a creature
that is very human-like.
They love to sing, and dance, and play--
some even ride a bike.

H

The Hippopotamus

The Hippo is an herbivore--
its dinner, a delight.
Some 80 pounds of grass is what
it eats most every night.

H

The Horned-Lizard

A scary-looking lizard
with its pointed horns and scales,
Sharp claws and many other strange
and frightening details.
And though it does look menacing,
it scares me not at all.
The reason--it is very, very,
very, very small.

H

The Horse

This sightless Appaloosa,
is named Ward the *Wonder Horse*.
His closest friend? A donkey,
the "seeing-eyed" of course.

The Horseshoe Crab

The horseshoe crab's big claim to fame,
Is clear and quite succinct.
Surviving an event that made
The dinosaur extinct.

I

Ivory-Billed Woodpecker

Too bad that Mr. Woody's
such a noisy little bird.
As is said about some children,
They are better seen than heard.

I

Ibex   **Ibis**

The Ibex and Ibis
sound practically the same.
And both will come in handy--
that's if Scrabble is the game.

J

The Jabiru

In birds that fly, you'll find this is
the tallest of them all.
Without its shoes, it measures
an impressive five feet tall

J

Jackson's Chameleon

Whether sunning on the rocks
or maybe sleeping in a tree,
Its skin of many colors
is a bare necessity.

The Kinkajou

Two special things have made
the Kinkajou complete.
A tongue that's really very long
and reversible hind feet.

Komodo Dragon

The world would be a better place
without this dinosaur.
A lizard or a dragon.
Who needs either anymore?

L

The Llama

The Llama is unusual.
Its name is hard to spell.
It's easy to forget that it
begins with double L.

M

The Macaroni Penguin

The Macaroni Penguin--
yellow feathers on its top.
While penguins mostly waddle,
macaroni penguins hop!

N

The Nautilus

The Nautilus--a cross between
an octopus and squid.
I never ever tasted one.
I never ever did.

O

The Ocelot
In the market for a kitten--
please forget the ocelot.
They look so cute and cuddly,
but they certainly are not.

O

The Orangutan

Regarding the orangutan,
One fact we can't escape.
We all may be related to
This ginger-colored ape!

The Owl

The Owl--a raptor considered quite wise,
has one limitation--It can't move its eyes.
It gets along nicely, by using, instead,
A flexible neck and a swiveling head.

P

The Pelican

"A wonderful bird is the pelican.
His bill can hold more than his belly can.
He can take in his beak, enough food for a week.
But I'm darned if I see how the hell it can."

The Queensland Grouper

If you're feeding an army
for dinner tonight,
Then two of these fish
would be just about right.

R

Regal Jumping Spider

This fuzzy arachnid
has four sets of eyes.
Jim Henson's new Muppet?
I'd not be surprised.

R

Royal Amazon Flycatcher

Is there any other creature
that might possibly compare
To all these yellow feathers
and this multi-colored hair?

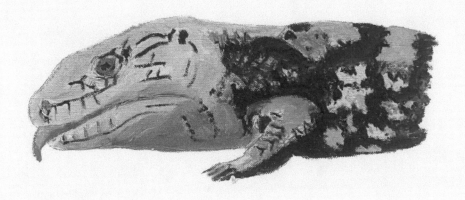

The Blue-tongued Skink

You may have guessed by now,
this is the blue-tongued skink.
I do believe--If you'd prefer
they also come in pink.

The Stoplight Loosejaw

Beware this deep-sea dragon fish.
A creepy-looking guy.
With red and green lights shining
brightly underneath each eye.

T

Tenrec

I've never seen the Tenrec.
It's a porcupine of sorts.
That may be because it sleeps all day,
according to reports.

The Unau

Two things about the Unau
Just in case you didn't know,
The first is that it's lazy,
The second--it is slow!

The Urial

While this ram might be included
in the Chinese Zodiac,
It could serve a better purpose as
the perfect two-hat rack.

The Vampire Bat

Last night I had a visit
from this flying vampire bat.
Perhaps it's time for me to get
a hungry pussy cat.

The Vulture

A bird of prey, the Vulture,
has no feathers on its head.
They're known for eating anything,
As long as it is dead.

The Wallaby

The Wallaby or Wallaroo--
Australian kangaroos.
There is very little difference
in whichever you might choose.
Though scientists suggest that they
would make the perfect pet,
I don't believe I'm ready for
a Wallaby just yet.

The Warthog

Describing the Warthog--
we all should agree,
This beast is as ugly
as ugly can be.

The Xanado   **The Xanadon't**

This Xanado creature--
the perfect mascot.
Its cousin the Xanadon't--
certainly not!

The Yellow-banded Poison Dart Frog

If you found one in your garden,
best not keep it as a pet.
It would be a bad decision;
one you'll certainly regret.
One of earth's most deadly creatures.
Get a hamster or a mouse!
But **never** let this froggy
set one foot inside your house!

The Zebu

You'll never find some Zebu
on a Hindu dinner plate.
Although its meat might prove to be
the best they ever ate.
The reason--it's revered by every Hindu
and their spouse.
So, Zebu beef is never served
in any Hindu house.